MACMILLAN

COLOUR DICTIONARY

Jeff Bevington

Illustrated by
Peter Bailey
Ann Baum
Peter Dennis
Tony Morris
Trevor Parkin

M
Macmillan Education

HOW TO FIND THE WORD YOU WANT

The words in this book are in alphabetical order.

Words with **a** as their first letter come first. You will find them on pages 4 and 5.

Then come words which have **b** as their first letter. They are on pages 6 — 8. Then come words with **c** as the first letter, then **d**, and so on to **z**.

If you know your alphabet, you can do these puzzles.

1 Write the letters which are left out of these lines, and you will find that you have written five words:

a)   a cdefghijk mn pqrstuv xyz
b)   abc efgh jklmnopq s uvwx z
c)   abcd fghijkl no qrs uvwx z
d)   abcde gh jklmnopq   uvwxyz
e)   abcdefghij lm   pqrstuv xyz

2 Now put these colours in alphabetical order:

yellow	violet	blue	orange
green	silver	red	white

3 Look at pages 6 and 7 in this dictionary.
Why does b<u>a</u>d come before b<u>e</u>d?

4 Look at page 7.
Why does bi<u>c</u>ycle come before bi<u>r</u>d?

5 Look at page 9.
Why does br<u>ot</u>her come before br<u>ow</u>n?

HOW TO FIND THE WORD YOU WANT

6 Now look at the words in the boxes.
Which one comes first? Why?

a) | bag
    | big

b) | bed
    | bear

c) | more
    | moon

d) | tall
    | talk

7 Write these words in alphabetical order:
a) throw   take   twenty   today
b) moon   money   mouse   morning
c) white   wheel   where   what

8 Now put these names in alphabetical order. If you have done it correctly, the names will go from the smallest thing to the biggest one.
a) elephant   cat   donkey   acorn
b) lion   glove   moon   hat
c) train   saw   shirt   table
d) kitchen   kite   key   lorry

9 Here are words from pages 43 and 44 of this book. Write them in alphabetical order. Do not look!

sneeze   smoke   sing   sky   snake
small   sister   soft   sit   slow
skirt   skip
Were you right?

So that this book will help you as much as possible, you will see that all the nouns are printed in red, all the adjectives are printed in blue and all the verbs are printed in green.

3

Aa

aeroplane

The **aeroplane** is on the ground.

about (1)

This is a story **about** a giant.

about (2)

There are **about** twenty birds in the field.

afternoon

The boys played football in the **afternoon**.

acorn

Tom looks for **acorns** on the oak tree.

again

Sam has cut his knee **again**.

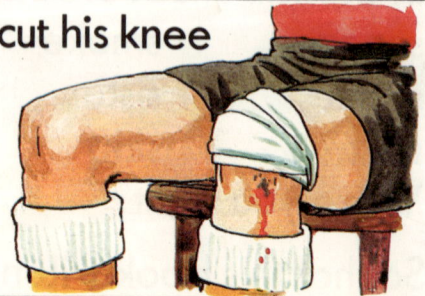

across

Jenny ran **across** the road.

all

The children are **all** girls.

alphabet

Mary writes the **alphabet** in big letters and small letters.

ABCDEFGHIJKLMNOPQRSTUVWXYZ

abcdefghijklmnopqrst

ambulance

Grandma went in an **ambulance**.

angry

The farmer is **angry** with the boys.

animals

These are all **animals**.

apple

Ted is eating a red **apple**.

arm

The girl has broken her **arm**.

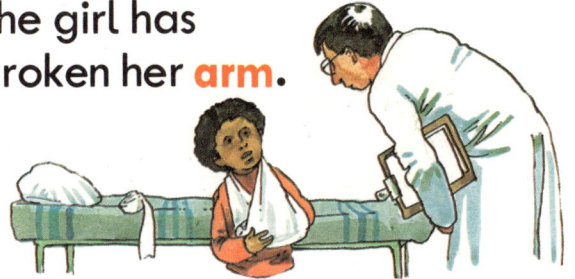

asleep

The old man is **asleep**

awake

Now the baby is **awake**.

away

John ran **away** from the bear.

Bb

baby

The **baby** sleeps in her cot.

bad (1)

This apple is **bad**.

bad (2)

Mother said Tim was a **bad** boy.

bag

Sue has a pretty **bag**.

ball

Jack likes to play with a **ball**.

bat (1)

This **bat** can hit a ball.

bat (2)

This **bat** can fly.

bath

The children are in the **bath**.

6

be

Richard is going to **be** a fireman.

before

Wash your hands **before** you eat.

beach

Shells are found on the **beach**.

bicycle

Have you got a **bicycle**?

beautiful

The princess is **beautiful**.

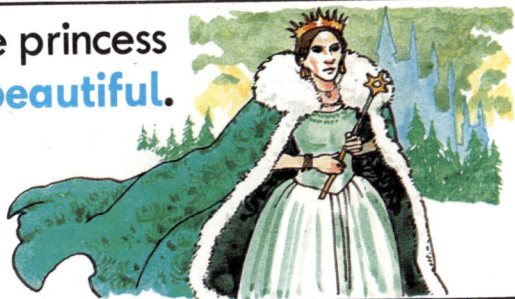

big

Dick has a **big** kite.
Tom's kite is **bigger**.
Sam's kite is the **biggest**.

bed (1)

Mary sleeps in this **bed**.

bed (2)

Grandad is weeding his flower **bed**.

bird

This little **bird** is a robin.

7

birthday

Susie is four today.
It is her **birthday**.

black

A **black** cat sat
by the wall.

blue

Our house has a **blue** door.

book

This is a **book** of stories.

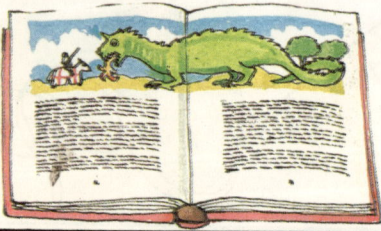

box

Which **box** has shoes in it?
Count the **boxes**.

boy

David is a big **boy**.

bread

Brown **bread** is good for you.

break

It will **break**
if you drop it!

Now it is **broken**!

brick

This house is made
of **bricks**.

8

brother

Tony is Katie's **brother**.

brown

The leaves are turning **brown**.

bus

Sarah goes to school on the **bus**.

butterfly

The **butterfly** is on a flower.

buy

Here is a toy shop.
You can **buy** lots of toys here.

Cc

cake

This is a sweet **cake**.

call (1)

"What do you **call** your dog?"
"His name is Rover."

call (2)

"Then please **call** Rover off the grass."

9

can (1)

There is petrol in that **can**.

can (2)

Gillian **can** skip well
but Jessie **cannot** (**can't**).

car

This is an old **car**.

cat

The **cat** is playing with
a ball of string.

chair

That **chair** has a broken leg.

child

Vijay is five.
He is a **child**.

Two other **children**
are playing with him.

clean

Are your teeth **clean**?
See how Mary **cleans** hers.

climb

These bears
can **climb** trees.

clock

The **clock** strikes
twelve.

coat

Sally has a new **coat** for the winter.

colour

What **colour** are the cat's eyes?

come

Sam said, "**Come** to my party."

All the children **came**.

count

Ted can **count** in threes. Can you?

3,6,9,

cow

A **cow** gives milk.

Dd

dance

Emily likes to **dance**. She is **dancing** round and round.

dark

The sky is **dark** before rain.

day (1)

Owls fly at night and sleep by **day**.

day (2)

The **days** of the week are:

MONDAY TUESDAY WEDNESDAY THURSDAY FRIDAY SATURDAY SUNDAY

11

deep - donkey

deep

Don't go in
the **deep** end!

2 m

dig

Tom helps Dad to **dig**.
He likes **digging**.
He has **dug** up
the roots.

dinner

Pippa has **dinner** at school.
Do you?

dirty

Look how **dirty** that car is!

do

"When will you **do**
your painting, John?"
"I am **doing** it now."

Do you like the painting?
John **did**.
I **do**. He **does**.

dog

Mandy takes her **dog**
for a walk.

doll

Nicola's **doll**
has blue eyes.

donkey

The **donkey** has
big ears.

12

door

This **door** is made of oak.

dress (1)

Julie puts on her pink **dress**.

down (1)

Jack fell **down** the hill.

dress (2)

She is **dressing** to go to a party.

down (2)

Polly wrote **down** the answer.

drink

Our cat likes to **drink** milk.

draw

Claire likes to **draw**. She has **drawn** a witch.

drop (1)

A **drop** of rain ran down the pane.

drop (2)

Don't **drop** that jug!

But he **dropped** it!

13

ear - eye

Ee

ear

John put his fingers in his **ears.**

egg

All these animals lay **eggs.**

eight

A spider has **eight** legs.

elephant

Have you had a ride on an **elephant**?

eleven

There are **eleven** eggs in the nest.

empty

There is no more to drink. The glass is **empty.**

ever

Have you **ever** seen a witch?

every

Is there an apple for **every** boy?

eye

Jessie has a fly in her **eye.**

Ff

face (1)

The baby has jam on its **face**.

face (2)

The man turned to **face** the lion.

fall

Dad saw the aeroplane **fall**. It **fell** into the sea.

farm

This is a **farm**.

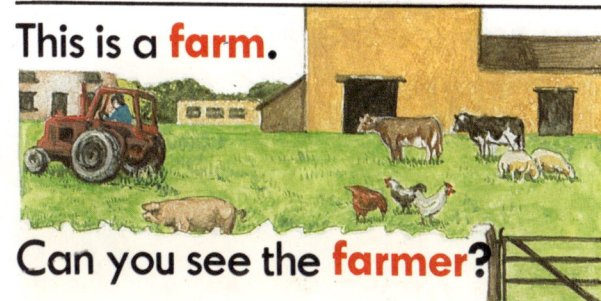

Can you see the **farmer**?

fast

This is a **fast** car.

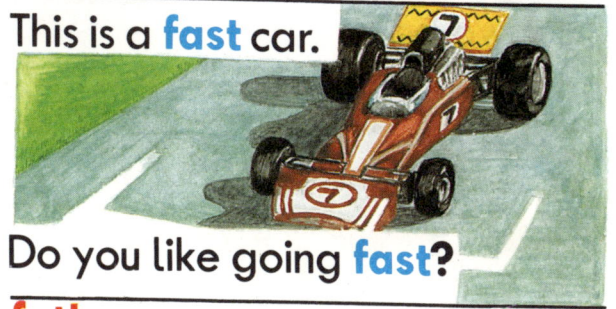

Do you like going **fast**?

father

Jill's **father** waves to her.

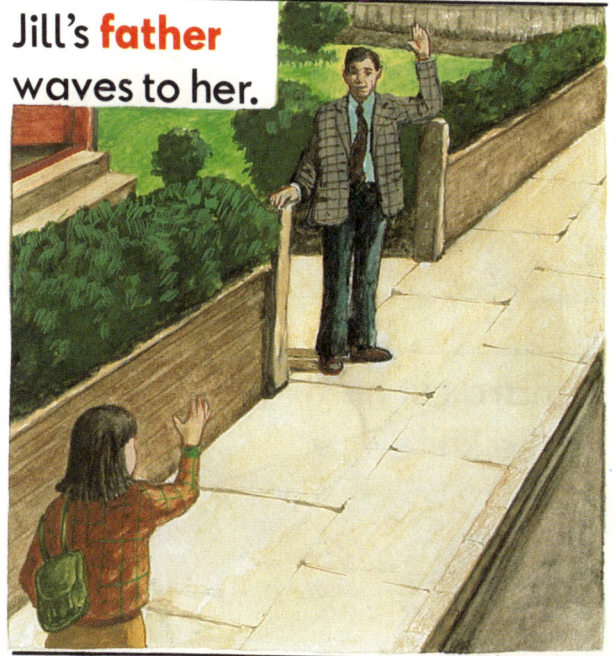

feel

Does the water **feel** cold?

fetch

The dog ran to **fetch** the ball.

15

fight - flower

fight (1)

The two boys had a **fight**.

fight (2)

That little dog will **fight** the big one.

finger

Richard cut his **finger** on the knife.

fire

Help! The house is on **fire**!

The **firemen** came quickly.

first

Jill came **first** in the race.

fish (1)

What is this **fish** called?

fish (2)

Dad is going to **fish** in the river.

five

Here are **five** numbers. What are they?

7 13 21 99 17

flower

You can see these **flowers** in summer.

16

fly (1)

There is a **fly** on John's cap.
He does not like **flies**.

fly (2)

This bird can **fly** fast.

Watch it **flying**.

foot

This is a horse's **foot**.

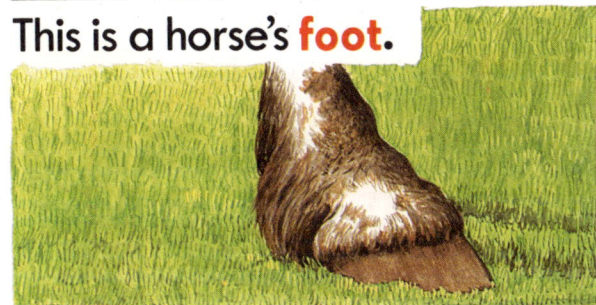

Which animals have these **feet**?

fork

One **fork** is for eating.
One **fork** is for digging.

four

Our dog had **four** puppies.

friend

Joan and Doreen are **friends**.

frog

Watch the **frog** jump!

front

The **front** of the house
is white.

funny

The hippopotamus looks **funny**
in a hat!

Gg

game

What **game** are these children playing?

garage

The **garage** sells oil and petrol.

gate

Bob swings on the **gate**

get

Did Jim **get** wet?

Yes, he **got** very wet!

giant

The **giant** held the man in his hand.

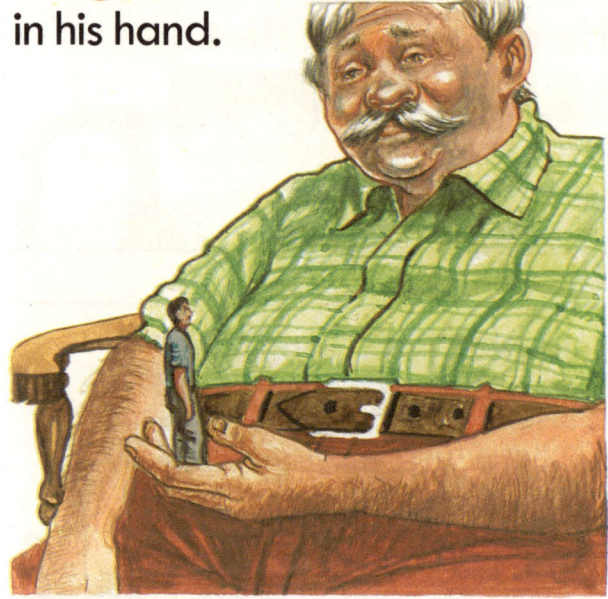

girl

Jackie is a pretty **girl**.

give

What did Liz **give** to Nigel?

She **gave** him a toy helicopter.

glass

Tom upset his **glass** of water.

go

The children **go** to the beach.
Father **goes** to fetch a chair.
Mary is **going** to swim.
Billy has **gone** to dig.

good

Eric is a **good** boy.

Grandmother/Grandfather

Grandmother and **Grandfather** have grey hair.

grass

The donkey is eating the **grass**.

greedy

That dog is **greedy**!

green

How **green** the leaves are!

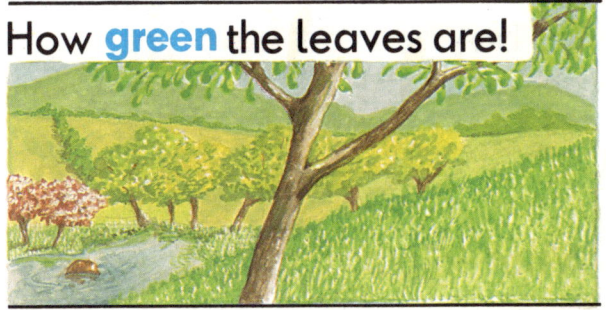

grey

The doctor has a **grey** coat.

gun

The big **gun** made a loud noise.

Hh

hair

This boy has red **hair**.

What colour is yours**?**

half

Sam cut the cake in **half**.

You can write '**half**' like this: **½**

hand

Marie held the ball in her **hand**.

handkerchief

Linda has a pretty **handkerchief**.

happy

Richard is **happy**. He is dancing.

hard

Oak is a very **hard** wood.

hat

Which **hat** do you like?

have

What books **have** you got? Hetty **has** these.

head (1)

The bird has a blue top to its **head.**

head (2)

Watch him **head** the ball.

hear

Sam likes to **hear** the birds singing.

Have you **heard** them?

heavy

That clock is **heavy.**

helicopter

The man was rescued by **helicopter.**

help

Emily **helps** to catch the horse.

here

It is very cold **here.**

hide

The mouse **hides** under the hay. It is **hiding** from the cat.

Can you see where it is **hidden?**

high

The balloon is **high** in the sky.

21

hit - hurt

hit

Richard **hit** the ball over the wall.

hold

This is how you should **hold** a bird.

horse

This **horse** can run very fast.

hot

Don't touch the fire. It's **hot**!

house

Have you ever seen a **house** like this?

how

Mum shows Micky **how** to make pastry.

hundred

Ten times ten makes a **hundred** Is that right?

$$10 \times 10 = 100$$

hungry

The birds are **hungry** in winter.

hurt

Tom fell over and **hurt** his knee.

Ii

I

"**I** can stand on my head,"
said Mary.

ice

That **ice** is very thin.

You can eat these **ices**.

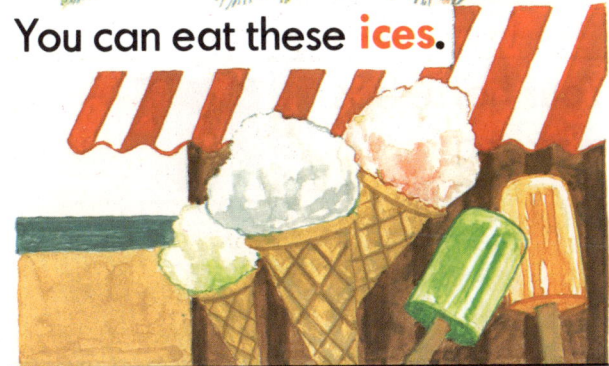

if

Rosemarie will fall **if**
she climbs up there.

ill

Frank is **ill** in bed.

in

The rabbit is **in** the hutch.
Don't let it out!

into

The children ran
into the sea.

is

Richard **is** Rachael's brother.
They are twins.

it

"Do you like cake?"
"Yes, I like **it** very much."

Jj

jam

Which **jam** do you like?

joke

He put on a funny nose as a **joke**.

jug

This **jug** is blue and white.

jump

Can a cow **jump** over the moon?

Kk

keep

Charlie **keeps** his bike in the garage.

key

This is the **key** to the front door.

kick (1)

Your horse has a strong **kick**!

kick (2)

Tim **kicks** the ball and Ben stops it.

kitchen

Dad is washing up in the **kitchen**.

kite

Ted is flying his **kite** on the hill.

knee

Help Grandma. She has a bad **knee**.

knife

That **knife** is very sharp.

Do not play with **knives**.

Ll

last

Jack ate the **last** cake.

laugh

The children **laugh** at the show.

leaf

This **leaf** is from an oak tree.

There are many **leaves** on it.

leave

Father **leaves** the money on the table.

Can you see where he **left** it?

left

The car turned **left** at the crossroads.

leg

My horse hurt its **leg** at the water jump.

let

The policeman will not **let** the boy go.

letter

Jim put the **letter** in the pillar box.

These are **letters** too: **A B C D**

library

Rebecca got a book from the **library**.

lift (1)

The **lift** goes up to the top.

lift (2)

John can **lift** the heavy bag.

light (1)

The **light** shines over the sea.

light (2)

The seeds are so **light**, they blow in the wind.

like (1)

Susie is **like** her mother.

like (2)

Ted does not **like** oranges.

listen

Listen to the noise
the dogs are making!

little

The baby held out its
little hands.

live

These animals **live** in woods.

look

The children **look**
at the animals.

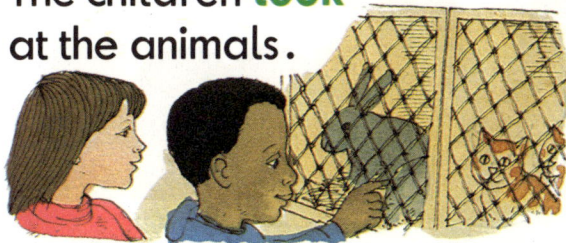

lorry

That **lorry** has big wheels.

lose

"Don't **lose** that, Brian."

But Brian **lost** it.

loud

Please turn the radio down.
It's much too **loud**!

Mm

make

Mother helps Ben to **make** a model.

man

One **man** rode on a horse and two **men** went on foot.

many

There are too **many** cars on the road.

measure

Can you **measure** from A to B?

A ←⎯⎯⎯⎯→ B

meet

Mother goes to **meet** Keith from school.

mend

Can you **mend** my bike, please?

middle

The puppy dug a hole in the **middle** of the lawn.

milk

Gillian drinks a glass of **milk**.

mix

The twins help to **mix** a cake.

morning

They saw a fox in the **morning**.

monkey

The baby **monkey** holds on to its mother.

mouse

This **mouse** has a very long nose.

Some **mice** sleep all winter.

moon

Look at this **moon**. What shape is it?

much

Susie has too **much** potato!

more

many birds

more birds

the **most** birds

music

That dog sings when he hears **music**!

Nn

nail

Can you hit a **nail** into wood?

Don't hit your finger**nail**!

narrow

The river is so **narrow** you could jump across.

naughty

It was **naughty** of Steven to pull his sister's hair.

near

The cat likes to sit **near** the fire.

nest

How many eggs are in the **nest**?

new

John had a **new** bicycle for his birthday.

nine

There are **nine** stones in the ring.

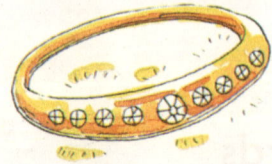

night

Day is over
Now it is **night**.

nobody

The people have gone.
There is **nobody** on the beach.

noise

Which of these makes
a very loud **noise**?

nose

Which animal has got
a long **nose**?

not

Is that man a policeman?
No, he is **not**.

number

1 3 5 21 99

These are all **numbers**.

Oo

oak

King Charles hid
in an **oak** tree.

of

A bag **of** potatoes is by
the door **of** the house.

off

Please take your dirty
shoes **off**.

often

Grandpa **often** loses his
glasses.

31

old

This church is 100 years **old**.

How **old** are you?

on

Sheila's dress is **on** the chair.

She is going to put it **on**.

one

The giant had **one** eye.

only

There are three children, but **only** two sweets!

open

John runs to **open** the gate.

orange (1)

Bill is eating an **orange**.

orange (2)

Sally has an **orange** balloon.

out

The bird flew **out** of the nest.

outside

There is a big van **outside** the house.

over (1)

The helicopter flew **over** the school.

over (2)

The men crossed **over** the river.

over (3)

The sun is coming out — the rain is **over**.

owl

A white **owl** hooted loudly.

Pp

paint (1)

The **paint** is by the door.

paint (2)

Cheryl **paints** the door blue.

paper

This bag is made of strong **paper**.

park (1)

There are swings in the **park**.

33

park (2)

Father **parks** the car
by the river.

party

Karen and Leo
are at a **party**.

pass (1)

Please **pass** the sandwiches.

pass (2)

Will the horse
pass the donkey?

pea

Ali helps to shell the **peas**.

pear

Tony is eating a **pear**.

Half of it is bad.

pen

Do you write with a
pen like this?

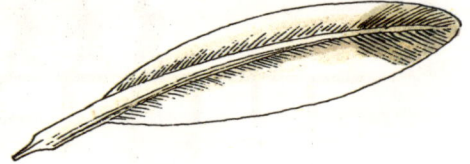

pencil

Tom likes to draw
with a sharp **pencil**.

penny

Bill has a new **penny**.
Ian has some old **pennies**.

people

Lots of **people** are
watching the game.

petrol

The car stops at the garage
for **petrol**.

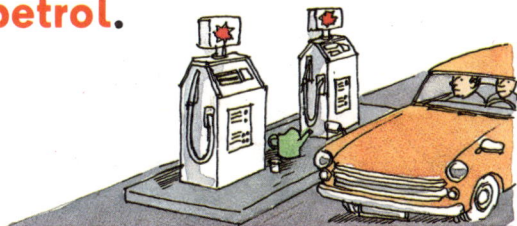

pet

What animal would you
like as a **pet**?

picture

There is a **picture**
on the wall.

pig

This **pig** is hungry.

pillow

The cat sleeps
on the **pillow**.

pin

Ben stood on a **pin**!

play

Tim likes to **play**
with the bricks.

pocket

The man took a key
from his **pocket**.

policeman

The **policeman** hid behind the door.

potato

Dan ate a boiled **potato**.

Do you like **potatoes**?

pretty

All these dolls are **pretty**.

prince/princess

The **prince** helped the **princess** on to her horse.

pull

The girls **pull** the boat up the beach.

puppet

Jean made this **puppet**.

puppy

The naughty **puppy** has eaten Julie's doll.

push

The man has to **push** the wheelbarrow.

put

Dad **put** the book on his desk.

Qq

quack

The ducks **quack** as they swim.

quarrel

The children **quarrel** about the toys.

quarter

Cut the cake into four, and there will be a **quarter** for each child.

You can write one '**quarter**' like this: $\frac{1}{4}$

queen

Listen to the cheers as the **queen** comes out!

question

You often ask **questions**, like:

What is that for?

What is it made of?

Why is it that funny shape?

Where does it come from?

You write ? to show that a sentence is a **question**.

quite

The jug is not **quite** empty.

quiet

We are **quiet** when the teacher comes in.

Rr

rabbit

Adrian has a pet **rabbit**.

radio

Fay turned on her **radio**.

rain (1)

The drops of **rain** ran down the window.

rain (2)

The sky is dark. It is going to **rain**.

rainbow

Now there is a **rainbow** over the hill.

rat

The **rat** ran under the barn.

read

Jessica likes to **read** in bed.

What is she **reading**?

red

Jack has a cold. His nose is **red**.

38

ride

Jeremy can **ride** well.

right (1)

You take the first turn on the **right** to get to the river.

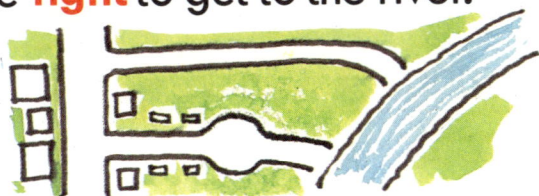

right (2)

It's nice when you get your sums **right**!

$$\begin{array}{r} 1\,0 \\ 1\,2 \\ \hline 2\,2 \end{array} + \quad \checkmark$$

ring (1)

Gran has three **rings** on her fingers.

ring (2)

The bell is going to **ring** now.

river

Look at all the fish in the **river**!

road

Does the **road** wind up the hill?

rock (1)

Tony sits on the **rock** by the sea.

rock (2)

The waves **rock** the ship.

roof

The fireman climbed on the **roof**.

round (1)

The bicycle's wheels are **round**.

round (2)

The top whirrs as it goes **round**.

rub

If you **rub** hard, it will shine.

Keep on **rubbing**!

run

This animal can **run** very fast.

Look at it **running** away.

Ss

sad

This doll looks happy

but that one looks **sad**.

sail

This ship can **sail** out to sea.

Can you see the **sailors**?

sand

The **sand** is full of shells.

sandal

Betty has lost one **sandal**.

say

What do you **say** when you get a present?

John **said**, "Thank you."

sandwich

This is a jam **sandwich**.

Do you like **sandwiches**?

school

Ann goes to this **school**.

saucer

The cat has her milk in a **saucer**.

scissors

These **scissors** are for cutting paper.

sausage

The naughty dog took a **sausage** from the shop.

sea

There are big waves on the **sea**.

saw

Father cuts the wood with a **saw**.

see

Can you **see** with your eyes shut?

41

seed - sheep

seed

The flower **seed** is on the table.

shape

What do you call this **shape**?

see-saw

Do you like to go up and down on a **see-saw**?

sharp

That knife is very **sharp**!

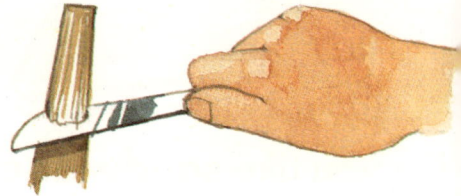

send

The shop **sends** the furniture by van.

she

That is the mother bear. **She** is playing with her cub.

shallow

You can walk across the **shallow** river.

sheep

All the **sheep** are in the pen.

42

shell

This **shell** is a pretty shape.

shine

The sun **shines** when the rain is over.

ship

The **ship** is in deep water.

shirt

Do you like Jan's new **shirt**? It is a T-**shirt**.

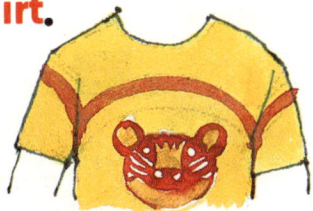

show

Celia **shows** the children her new ring.

sick

Leo has eaten too many sweets. They have made him **sick**.

sing

Listen to the robin **singing**. He has a pretty **song**.

sister

Jennie is very like her **sister**.

sit

Can an elephant **sit** down?

Yes! It **sat** on a tub!

skip

Emma can **skip** well. She has a new **skipping** rope.

43

skirt

Gwen is making a **skirt**.

sky

The **sky** was red as the sun went down.

slow

The car is passing the **slow** lorry.

small

These birds are very **small**. What are they?

smoke

There is **smoke** coming from the chimney.

snake

Can you see a **snake** in the tree?

sneeze

Use a handkerchief if you **sneeze**.

snow

The children are playing in the **snow**.

It is **snowing** again now.

44

soap

Harry is dirty.
He washes with **soap**.

spell

Can you **spell** well?

socks

Olga puts on her green **socks**.

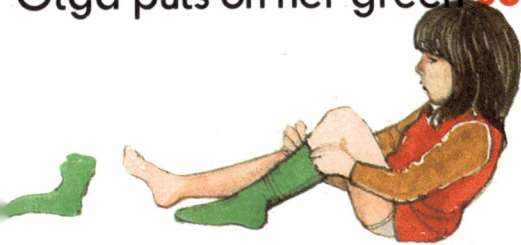

spider

A big **spider** ran across
the bath.

soft

Feel how **soft** the pillow is.

spot

Ken has **spots** all over him.

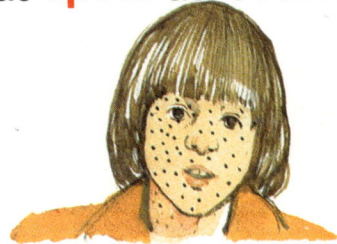

some

Hanif has **some**
coloured pencils.

square

This is a **square**.

stairs

Those **stairs** go
right to the top.

stamp

Rebecca put a **stamp** on the letter.

stand

Stand still while I take your photograph.

stone

The **stone** walls keep in the sheep.

stop

The warden put up his hand to **stop** the car.

Now it has **stopped**.

story

Mother reads a **story** to me. Do you read **stories** too?

strong

An elephant is very **strong**.

sum

The **sum** of 3 and 2 is 5. What is the **sum** of 4 and 3?

summer

In **summer**, the sun is hot.

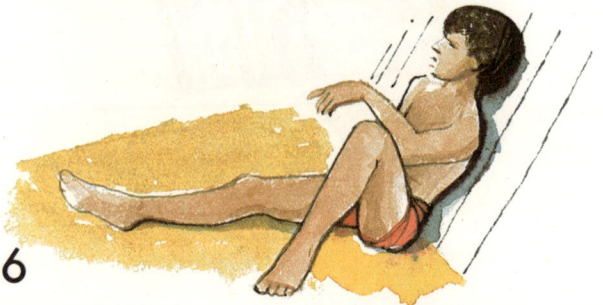

sun

He wears dark glasses in the **sun**.

Tt

sweets

Too many **sweets** are bad for you.

table

The children sit at the **table**.

swim

The fish open their mouths as they **swim**.

take

"Did Bill **take** his medicine?"

"Yes, he **took** it."

swing

The children have a **swing** to play on.

tall

How **tall** those men are!

They like **swinging**. Do you?

47

tea

Sarah pours a cup of **tea**.

teacher

Mrs. Brown is a good **teacher**.
She **taught** the children to read.

television

What programmes do you like
on **television**?

tell

John asked his dad to **tell**
him a story.
His dad **told** him about a sailor
called Sinbad.

ten

There are **ten** horses at the farm

5 + 5 = 10

thank

Charlie **thanks** his father
for his new bicycle.

that

Valerie likes **that** doll
in the toy shop.

their(s)

They get milk from **their** cows.
The Jersey cows are **theirs**.

then

They will meet at 2 o'clock and go swimming **then.**

there

Look at the duck over **there.**

they/them

Vic does not like flies. **They** are dirty. Do you like **them?**

thick

Bill has a **thick** sandwich.

thin

What a **thin** boy he is!

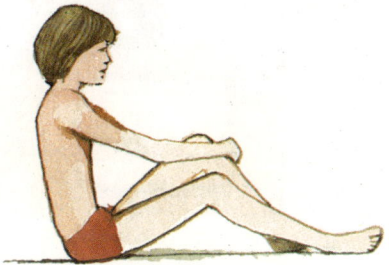

thing

Joe helps to put the **things** away in the kitchen.

this

This animal is tall.

These animals are short.

three

Nancy drew **three** ducks.

throw

Donna **throws** a stone into the sea.

49

tie (1)

Jim has a green **tie** with yellow spots.

tie (2)

Can you **tie** a knot like this?

time

What is the **time**?
Nine o'clock — **time** for school.

tired

Bob is **tired**. He has walked a long way.

today

David is ten years old **today**. It is his birthday.

toes

Can you dance on your **toes** like this?

too

That is **too** big to get in!

tooth

The baby is cutting a **tooth**. She has three **teeth** now.

top

The cat is on **top** of the television.

touch

Do not **touch** this animal.

toy

Ben is playing with his **toys**.

tractor

What is this **tractor** pulling?

train (1)

The **train** is going very fast.

train (2)

You can **train** a dog
to fetch sheep.

tree

This **tree** does not
lose its leaves in winter.

triangle

This is a **triangle**.

tricycle

Eric's **tricycle** has
lost a wheel.

true

Is it **true** that some
birds can talk?

I CAN TALK!

trunk

The elephant blows water on its back with its **trunk**.

twenty

There are **twenty** houses in the street.

turn (1)

Take the **turn** to the right by the shop.

twins

Jane and Bob are **twins**.

turn (2)

Please **turn** on the radio.

two

Look at the owl's **two** big eyes.

twelve

Twelve eggs stand in the box.

tyres

The car's **tyres** are too soft. Dad is pumping them up.

Uu

umbrella

That man's **umbrella** blew away!

uncle

Tom's mother has a brother called Jeff. He is Tom's **uncle**.

under

Mick is hiding **under** the bed.

untidy

The children's room is very **untidy**!

up

The kitten climbed **up** the tree.

upside-down

Sally likes to be **upside-down**. She can stand on her head.

upstairs

Mother opens all the windows **upstairs**.

us

We are hiding. Can you find all five of **us**?

Vv

van

The policemen stopped the **van**.

vegetable

Can you name all these **vegetables**?

very

That car is going **very** fast.

violet

Pam found these **violets** in a wood.

violin

Peter plays his **violin** every day.

voice

The singer has a loud **voice**.

volcano

Fire and smoke come out of the **volcano**.

Ww

wait

The car **waits** for the lorry to cross.

walk

Katie took off her shoes to **walk** on the sand.

want

What does the dog **want**?

wash

Aziz takes the soap to **wash** his hands.

watch (1)

This **watch** keeps good time.

watch (2)

Tony likes to **watch** the birds.

water (1)

Give the flowers some **water**.

water (2)

Water them with a **watering**-can.

55

wave (1)

A big **wave** breaks on the beach.

wave (2)

Rachael shows the baby how to **wave**.

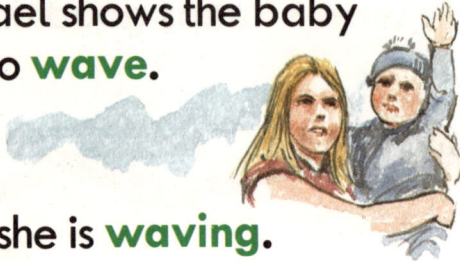

Now she is **waving**.

way

The mouse found its **way** to the zoo.

TO THE ZOO

we

We want to cross the road, but it is very busy.

wear

Donna will **wear** blue.

week

How many days are there in a **week**?

Sun	Mon	Tue	Wed	Thu	Fri	Sat
1	2	3	4	5	6	7
8	9	10	11	12	13	1

well (1)

Jim dropped a stone down the **well**.

well (2)

Valerie can swim **well** for her age.

went

The rabbit **went** on to the grass.

wet

There is **wet** paint on this door.

which

Which of these animals eats grass?

what

Do you know **what** this animal is?

white

The **white** cat has long fur.

when

It is hot **when** the sun comes out.

who

There is the man **who** mends chairs.

where

You can see **where** the balloon came down.

why

Why did the horse kick? Do you know **why?**

wide

·The river is too **wide** to cross.

will

The doctor **will** look at Nigel's cut finger.

wind

The **wind** blew down this tree.

window

The cat sits at the open **window**.

winter

There is snow on the ground in **winter**.

with

Jack is playing **with** his train.

wood (1)

There are many trees in this **wood**.

wood (2)

These things are made of **wood**

word

You have to make **words** in this game. Can you play it?

write

Mary likes to **write** stories. She is **writing** one about a princess.

58

Xx

x-ray

This is an **x-ray** picture of a hand.

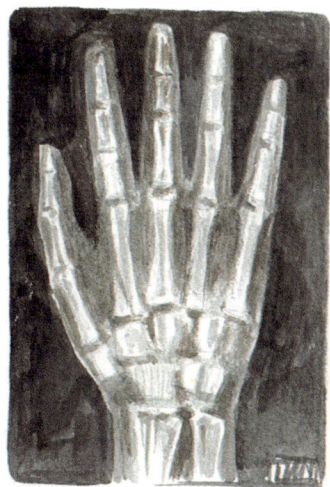

xylophone

Have you a **xylophone** like this at your school?

Yy

yawn

You **yawn** when you are tired.

year

Daniel is one **year** old today.

yellow

All these flowers are **yellow**.

yes

Are these oranges?
Yes, they are.

59

yesterday

It is Sunday today.
It was Saturday **yesterday**.

you

How old are **you?**

1 2 3 4 5 6 7
8 9 10 11 12

your

Jane's eyes are blue.
What colour are **your** eyes?

young

We call **young** dogs puppies.

What do we call **young** cats?

Zz

zebra

The **zebra** comes to
the water to drink.

zig-zag

The road turns this way and
that. It is a **zig-zag** road.

zip

Adrian's coat has a **zip**.

zoo

Most children like to go
to the **zoo**.

60

Days of the week

Sunday   Monday   Tuesday
Wednesday Thursday   Friday
           Saturday

Months of the Year

January   February   March
April   May   June
July   August   September
October   November   December

Seasons

Spring   Summer   Autumn   Winter

EXERCISES

1 Write these words in alphabetical order:

jersey	girl	chair	dirty	ice
fight	angry	heavy	eight	beautiful

2 These words begin with **g**. Write them in alphabetical order:

good   grass   gun   glass   get

3 Write these words in alphabetical order:

show   ship   shape   sheep

4 Write these words in alphabetical order:

stall   stamp   stand   stairs

Which letters did you look at?

5 Here are some children's names. Write them in alphabetical order:

Susan	Timothy	Amanda	Katherine	Pauline
Aziz	Leila	Janet	Gerald	Grace
Cary	Alex	Fatima	Elizabeth	Ahmed
Bernard	Trevor	Rebecca	Sylvia	Brian

6 How many words in this dictionary begin with the letter 's'?

7 Draw six big balloons. Write one of these letters, **A, B, M, P, T, W,** in each balloon. Now write the words from the lists in the right balloon. The first one is done for you. **Acorn** goes in the **A** balloon.

acorn	measure	today	pear	beautiful
week	paint	baby	ambulance	woman
teacher	window	more	television	watch
music	apple	play	brick	pencil
afternoon	meet	break	tractor	pillow
winter	blue	animals	tired	middle

EXERCISES

8 Write these sentences, putting in the word which has been left out. Use the dictionary to help you.
a) The f _ _ _ _ **of the house was white.**
b) There are n _ _ _ **stones in the ring.**
c) The car is passing the s _ _ _ **lorry.**
d) Adrian's new coat has a z _ _.
e) The princess is b _ _ _ _ _ _ _.

9 Write the word which means 'more than one' of these things:

one fly	two f
one foot	two f
one penny	two p
one story	two s
one child	two c
one puppy	two p
one knife	two k
one leaf	two l
one man	two m
one mouse	two m

10 Write the names of the days of the week. Look up the word 'day' in the dictionary if you are not sure how to spell them.

11 Write the words for these numbers:
1   4   8   2   9   12   11   20

12 Write the names of six colours.

13 Answer these questions from the dictionary.
a) Why did Katie take off her shoes?   (Look under Ww.)
b) What is Tom's uncle called?   (Look under Uu.)
c) What did Rebecca put on the letter?   (Look under Ss.)
d) Which animal is always hungry?   (Look under Pp.)

EXERCISES

e) You can eat with it or dig with it.   (Look under Ff.)
f) Who held a man in his hand?   (Look under Gg.)
g) Which animal ran under the barn?   (Look under Rr.)
h) Why is Jack's nose red?   (Look under Rr.)
i) What noise do ducks make?   (Look under Qq.)
j) Where do you go to buy petrol?   (Look under Gg.)

14 Fill in these missing words:
a) There are 26 l _ _ _ _ _ _ in the alphabet.
b) You have two, but a dog has four l _ _ _.
c) You put p _ _ _ _ _ in a car.
d) A t _ _ _ _ _ _ _ has three wheels.
e) Blue and yellow make g _ _ _ _.
f) Half of ten is f _ _ _.
g) Red and green are both c _ _ _ _ _ _.
h) 2 x 6 make t _ _ _ _ _.
i) If falls from the sky. It is white. It is s _ _ _.
j) You climb up to go u _ _ _ _ _ _ _.

15 Tomatoes, peas and potatoes are vegetables. What do you call apples, pears and oranges?

16 How many animals can you find in this dictionary? Birds, fish and insects are all animals, as well as cats and dogs. Make a picture with all the animals in.

17 Look in the dictionary. Write the words for all the things you can eat or drink.

© 1980 Jeff Bevington
Illustrations © 1980 Macmillan Education Ltd
First published 1980
Published by Macmillan Education Ltd
London and Basingstoke
Printed in Hong Kong